I AM NOT MY BEHAVIOR:
God Has A PURPOSE For ME

Elanena White

EJEM Blessings
Uplifting In Love
PO Box 10354
El Dorado,AR 71730

All scriptures from KJV or NIV

Inspiration for This Book

My goddaughter served as the book's inspiration. She goes by Toot, but her name is Neveah Byrd. She is a first grader who is 7 years old. She resides with Ruthie, her mother. Up until she was around 4 years old, Neveah led a typical life. When she first started acting out, it was later determined that she had attention deficit hyperactivity disorder (ADHD). ADHD is described as a chronic condition characterized by problems with concentration, hyperactivity, and impulsivity (2021). It is normal for children to have trouble focusing and behaving at one time or another. However, children with ADHD do not just grow out of these behaviors. The symptoms continue, can be severe, and can cause difficulty at school, at home, or with friends. Research does not support the popularly held views that ADHD is caused by eating too much sugar, watching too much television, parenting, or social and environmental factors such as poverty or family chaos (2021). Although the cause is uncertain, recent studies suggest that genetics may contribute.

Everyone adores Neveah because she is a joyful, kind, sweet, and spunky little girl. Currently, she is taking medication to help her manage her ADHD. She has control over it when she takes her medication. Before Neveah's mother realized what was going on, the teachers dubbed Neveah a naughty child and hounded her with calls, not realizing that Neveah had no influence over or comprehension of what was happening. Many times, people fail to see the child in favor of the behavior problem. Neveah is a cheerful kid at her current school and regarded as one of the best dressed. She enjoys creating tiktoks, posting photos on Facebook, and interacting with her followers. This book is dedicated to this sweet little girl. I appreciate her mother Ruthie Love for letting me tell a portion of her story.

Contents

Introduction

As a child, it can be tough to feel like you do not fit in or that your behavior is causing problems for yourself and those around you. It is not uncommon to feel misunderstood and frustrated without knowing where to turn to for help. This book offers guidance to help you better understand you and your behavior, and helps you develop a stronger relationship with God.

Our behavior is a reflection of our inner selves, and by improving our relationship with God, we can improve our personality, and our behavior.

One of the challenges that children with behavioral issues face is the stigma that often surrounds their behavior. They may be labeled as "bad kids" or "troublemakers," and this can create a negative cycle of self-doubt and low self-esteem. It is important for children to understand that their behavior does not define them, and that they are capable of change and growth.

This book is designed to help children understand that God has a purpose for their life, and that their behavior is an important part of that purpose. By learning how to manage their behavior and cultivate a positive relationship with God, children can unlock their full potential and become the best version of themselves.

Throughout the book, we will explore the ways in which faith and spirituality can support children in their journey towards better behavior. We will offer practical advice and guidance on how to manage difficult emotions, develop healthy habits, and find purpose and meaning in life. We will also discuss the importance of building a relationship with God and seeking his guidance and support.

By the end of this book, I hope that children will feel more empowered and equipped to manage their behavior and make positive changes in their lives. I encourage parents and mentors to read this book alongside their children and to offer support and guidance as they work towards their goals. Together, we can help children realize their full potential and live a purposeful and fulfilling life. I can accomplish anything through Christ who gives me strength, which is one of my favorite verses (Philippians 4:13). With this biblical perspective, we can make all things better so that God can receive the praise and so that we, you, and our children can begin to have healthier lives.

Chapter 1: Understanding Behavior and Emotions

In this chapter, we will explore the relationship between behavior and emotions, and help children understand how their behavior can reflect their inner selves.

What is Behavior?

Behavior is a way of acting or responding to the world around us. It can be positive or negative, depending on the situation and the individual's perception. Sometimes, behavior can be a deliberate choice, while other times it may be an automatic response to a stimulus.

Behavior is often influenced by a person's emotions, which can be influenced by many factors, including external events, physical sensations, and mental states.

Understanding Emotions

Emotions are a natural and important part of the human experience. They are the way we feel about different situations and can range from positive emotions like happiness and love to negative emotions like anger and fear.

It is important to understand that all emotions are valid and normal, but it is how we manage them that can make a difference in our behavior. Emotions can be powerful, and they can influence our behavior in both positive and negative ways.

For example, let us say you are feeling frustrated because you are having trouble with your math homework. If you manage your frustration in a positive way, you might take a break and come back to it later, or you might ask a friend for help. However, if you manage your frustration in a negative way, you might throw your pencil across the room or yell at your parents.

The Connection between Emotions and Behavior

Our emotions can have a direct impact on our behavior, and it is important to understand this connection. When we experience negative emotions, like anger or fear, we may be more likely to engage in negative behavior like yelling, hitting, or throwing things.

Nevertheless, it is important to remember that we can learn to manage our emotions and choose our behavior. We do not have to be controlled by our emotions. Instead, we can learn to recognize our emotions and respond to them in a positive and healthy way.

For example, if you are feeling angry, you might take a deep breath and count to ten before responding. On the other hand, if you are feeling sad, you might talk to a friend or family member about how you are feeling.

Recognizing and Managing Emotions

Recognizing Emotions

Recognizing our emotions is the first step in managing them. It is important to understand that all emotions are valid and normal, but sometimes it can be difficult to identify and express them.

One way to recognize our emotions is to pay attention to physical sensations in our bodies. For example, if you are feeling nervous, you might feel a fluttering in your stomach or sweaty palms. If you are feeling angry, you might feel your face getting hot or your fists clenching.

Another way to recognize emotions is to use "I" statements to describe how you are feeling. For example, "I feel sad because my friend canceled our plans," or "I feel happy because I got an A on my test."

Managing Emotions

Managing our emotions can be challenging, but it is an important skill to develop. By learning to manage our emotions, we can also improve our behavior and make positive choices that align with our values and goals.

Breathing Exercises

One technique for managing emotions is deep breathing exercises. By taking slow, deep breaths, we can calm our bodies and minds and reduce feelings of stress and anxiety.

To try deep breathing, find a quiet place to sit or lie down. Close your eyes and take a slow, deep breath in through your nose. Hold it for a few seconds, and then exhale slowly through your mouth. Repeat this process several times until you feel more relaxed.

Mindfulness and Meditation

Another technique for managing emotions is mindfulness and meditation. This involves focusing on the present moment and letting go of negative thoughts and emotions.

To try mindfulness, find a quiet place to sit or lie down. Close your eyes and focus on your breath, taking slow, deep breaths. If your mind starts to wander, gently bring your attention back to your breath.

Positive Affirmation

Positive affirmation can also be a helpful technique for managing emotions. This involves using positive, supportive language to encourage yourself and boost your confidence.

For example, if you are feeling nervous about a test, you might say to yourself, "I can do this. I've studied hard and I'm prepared." By using positive affirmation, you can reduce feelings of anxiety and boost your self-esteem.

Physical Exercise

Physical exercise is another great way to manage emotions. Exercise releases endorphins, which can boost your mood and reduce feelings of stress and anxiety.

You do not need to do a lot of exercise to feel the benefits. Even a short walk or some gentle stretching can be helpful.

Seeking Support

Finally, it is important to remember that it's okay to seek support from others when managing emotions. Talk to a trusted friend or family member, or seek help from a counselor or therapist if needed.

Chapter 2: Knowing Yourself

In Chapter 1, we talked about how behavior and emotions are connected. Nevertheless, it is important for children to understand that they are not their behavior. Their behavior is simply a response to something - whether it is a feeling, a need, or a desire.

Children with behavioral problems often feel like their actions define who they are. They may feel ashamed or embarrassed about their behavior, which can lead to feelings of low self-esteem and worthlessness. Oftentimes, they are labeled as "troublemakers" or "bad kids." However, the truth is, their behavior is just a symptom of something deeper going on.

For example, if a child is acting out in class, it could be because they are struggling with a difficult subject or feeling anxious about being around their peers. By understanding that your behavior is a response to something, you can begin to address the underlying issue and work towards improving their behavior.

One of the ways with which you can understand yourself is to reflect on your behavior. When you act out, ask yourself what might be causing that behavior. It may be that you are feeling angry, sad, frustrated, or trying to get attention.

You Are Not Your Behavior

It is important to understand that your behavior is not who you are. Your behavior is simply a response to something, such as a situation, emotion, or need. For example, if you are feeling stressed, you might snap at someone even though you do not mean to. It is important to recognize that this behavior does not define you as a person.

The ultimate thing you should know about yourself is that you are who God says you are. You may view yourself from you behavior or from what people say about you. However, these information are not the true picture of who you are. You need to find out who God says you are and reaffirm that to yourself repeatedly.

Reflecting On Your Behavior

Reflecting on your behavior can help you better understand your emotions, needs, and desires. Here are some questions to ask yourself when reflecting on your behavior:

What triggered my behavior? What was I feeling at the time?

Did my behavior help me get what I needed or wanted? Or did it make the situation worse?

How could I have responded differently? What other options did I have?

It is also important to ask yourself if you have certain intolerances. How do I react to noise in the market? or people poking fun at me?

By reflecting on your behavior, you can learn more about yourself and identify patterns or triggers that might lead to certain behaviors.

Understanding Your Emotions

In Psalm David expressed his most unsettling and unfavorable feelings. He often returned to what God accomplishes. You stitched me together in my mother's womb and created all the delicate, inner parts of my body. I appreciate you giving me such great complexity. How well I know that your work is excellent. Psalm 139:13-14 (NLT) God created you with great love and care. Similar to how He made everything lovely you see around you. You are a component of His magnificent creation.

Understanding your emotions is an important part of knowing yourself. Emotions can be complicated, but it is important to learn how to identify and express them in a healthy way. Here are some tips for understanding your emotions:

Name your emotions: Sometimes it can be difficult to identify what we are feeling. Try to name your emotions, such as happy, sad, angry, or anxious.

Recognize physical sensations: Emotions often come with physical sensations, such as a racing heart or butterflies in your stomach. Pay attention to these sensations to help identify what you are feeling.

Express your emotions: Expressing your emotions in a healthy way can help you process them and move forward. This might include talking to a trusted friend or family member, writing in a journal, or engaging in creative activities like drawing or music.

Tips for Identifying Triggers and Coping Mechanisms for Managing Difficult Situations.

Identifying triggers and developing coping mechanisms is an important part of managing difficult emotions and situations. Triggers are the thoughts or situations that lead to a certain response,in this case, negative responses. They could come from miscommunication, social misunderstanding, or sensory issues (stimuli). One of the key ways to identify these triggers is by observation, investigation, interaction, and perception.

Think about what triggers your negative emotions and behaviors. For example, if you struggle with anxiety, you may feel triggered in situations where there is a lot of noise or chaos. Once triggers have been identified, you can now begin to develop coping mechanisms that can help you manage their emotions in a healthy way (You may need to seek the help of an adult for this).

For example, if you are feeling anxious, you may benefit from deep breathing exercises or visualization techniques. Try to experiment with different coping mechanisms until they find one that works for them.

Coping with Difficult Emotions

By reflecting on your behavior, you can start to understand them better. You can identify patterns and triggers that might be causing you to act out. Moreover, most importantly, you can start to see that your behavior is not who you are.

Meditating on the word of God and prayer are powerful tools that can change your personality and behavior. Take time out every day to pray to God. Thank him for the gift of life, his loving-kindness and his mercy towards you. Remember to also talk to him about how you are feeling, asking for guidance in your daily activity.

By meditating on God's word, you will be more conscious of God and his word. This will help you to be more clearheaded, and you will be guided to react positively in different situations.

You can also practice journaling. Journaling is a great way for children to reflect on their thoughts and emotions. You can write about what happened during the day, how you felt about it, and what you could have done differently. This helps you process your emotions and identify patterns in your behavior.

Anger

Feeling angry is a normal and natural emotion, but it can be challenging to manage when it becomes overwhelming. Here are some strategies for coping with anger:

Practice forgiveness: Holding onto anger can be harmful to your emotional well-being. Practice forgiveness by letting go of grudges and focusing on positive thoughts and actions.

Take a break: If you feel yourself getting angry, take a break to cool down. Go for a walk; reflect on what you learnt from the word of God. You may practice deep breathing exercises.

Express your feelings: It is important to express your feelings in a healthy way. Talk to a trusted friend or family member about how you are feeling.

Anxiety

Anxiety is a feeling of unease or nervousness, often accompanied by physical symptoms such as a rapid heartbeat or sweating. Here are some strategies for coping with anxiety:

Prayer: when you are anxious, the best thing to do is to talk to God. By praying, you will release God's thought to your mind, an you will be able to conduct yourself well.

Practice mindfulness: Mindfulness involves focusing on the present moment and letting go of negative thoughts and emotions. Try deep breathing exercises or meditation to calm your mind and reduce feelings of anxiety.

Challenge negative thoughts: Anxiety can be fueled by negative thoughts and beliefs. Challenge these thoughts by questioning their validity and focusing on positive self-talk.

Engage in relaxing activities: Engage in activities that help you relax, such as reading a book, taking a warm bath, or practicing yoga.

Depression

Depression is a mood disorder that can cause feelings of sadness, hopelessness, and loss of interest in activities. Here are some strategies for coping with depression:

Reflect on the word of God: By reflecting on the word of God, you will remember that he loves you and that he cares for you. Meditating on god's word gives you peace, calmness and encouragement.

Talk to your parents or godly people: There is a saying that a problem shared is half-solved. When you talk to your parents, they can help you overcome it. Many times people keep depression to themselves that is why it slowly kills them. When you share it, you will be properly cared for.

Practice self-care: Practice self-care by engaging in activities that make you feel good, such as exercise, spending time with loved ones, or pursuing a hobby.

Challenge negative thoughts: Depression can be fueled by negative thoughts and beliefs. Challenge these thoughts with the thoughts of God about you. Think about positive things instead of negative things.

In summary, coping with difficult emotions such as anger, anxiety, and depression can be challenging, but it is important to develop strategies to manage them in a healthy way. By practicing mindfulness, challenging negative thoughts, engaging in relaxing activities, seeking help when needed, and practicing self-care, children can learn to cope with difficult emotions and make positive choices that align with their values and goals.

Chapter 3: God's Plan for Your Life

God cares about you, so your problems matter to Him. Oh God, how priceless are your thoughts for me. They are uncountable! They outnumber the sand grains; I can't even count them! And you'll still be there when I wake up! Psalm 139:17-18 (NLT) God is thinking a lot about you.

As a child, have you ever wondered what your purpose is in life? Maybe you feel like you do not have any direction or that you are not good at anything. But did you know that God has a plan for your life? It is true! He has a special purpose just for you, and it is up to you to discover what it is.

God has a plan for every child's life, and it is important to understand that this plan is good and beneficial, regardless of its behavior. It is easy to feel like our mistakes and missteps can derail us from fulfilling our purpose, but that is not how God works. He is always willing to guide us back on track, no matter how far we have strayed.

When you make mistakes or struggle with your behavior, do not give up. Remember that God loves you and is always there to help you. He forgives and gives the strength to do better. In addition, when you start living out God's plan for your life, you will find that it's an amazing adventure full of purpose and joy.

God's plan for your life is not just, about what you do, but also about who you are. He created you uniquely, with your own talents, interests, and personality. He wants you to use these gifts to bring glory to Him and to bless others. When you discover your purpose and start living it out, you will find a deep sense of fulfillment and joy.

So how can you discover God's plan for your life? It starts with seeking Him and listening to His voice. You can do this through prayer, reading the Bible, and spending time with other believers. Ask God to show you what He wants you to do and to give you the courage and strength to do it.

You can also think about your interests and talents. What are you naturally good at? What activities make you feel happy and fulfilled? These things can give you clues about what God might be calling you to do

It is also important to remember that you are not defined by your behavior. While your actions may affect the people around them, it does not change the fact that you are loved by God and have a purpose. You should never let your mistakes or struggles make you feel like they are unworthy of God's plan for their life.

Sometimes, it is hard to see the bigger picture when we are in the middle of a difficult situation. That is why it is important to trust in God's plan for our lives, even when things do not make sense. We may not always understand why we are going through a certain experience, but we can have faith that it is all part of God's plan.

When we trust in God's plan for our lives, we can let go of the worry and stress that often come with making decisions. Instead, we can focus on doing what are right and making choices that align with God's will. This can help us to avoid making poor choices that could hold us back from fulfilling God's plan for our lives.

Remember that discovering your purpose is a journey, not a destination. It is okay if you do not have all the answers right now. Just keep seeking God and taking steps in the direction He is leading you.

Finally, it is important to remember that God's plan for your life is not just about what you do, but also about whom you are becoming. He wants you to become more like Jesus, who was loving, kind, and selfless. This means treating others with respect, choosing kindness over anger, and striving to do your best in everything you do.

Chapter 4: Building a Relationship with God

In this chapter, we will talk about how faith and spirituality can offer children strength and support as they work to improve their behavior. We will also discuss how to develop a relationship with God through prayer, scripture, and other spiritual practices. Finally, we will explore the idea that God loves us unconditionally and offers us forgiveness and grace, even when we make mistakes.

Faith and Spirituality for Strength and Support

Faith and spirituality can provide a source of strength and support for children who are struggling with behavioral problems. By turning to God and their beliefs, children can find comfort and guidance in challenging times. They can also find a sense of purpose and direction in life, which can help them overcome their struggles.

One example of this is the story of a boy named Mark who was struggling with anger issues. He often lashed out at others and had trouble controlling his temper. However, after starting to attend church and learning about God's love and forgiveness, Mark began to feel more at peace with himself and his actions. He found comfort in prayer and began to make positive changes in his behavior.

Developing a Relationship with God

Developing a relationship with God is an important part of growing spiritually and emotionally. We can do this through prayer, reading scripture, attending church, and participating in other spiritual practices. By doing so, we can feel closer to God and understand His purpose for our lives.

One example of this is the story of a girl named Sarah who struggled with anxiety and self-doubt. She began to read the Bible and found comfort in the words of (Psalm 139), which reminded her that she was fearfully and wonderfully made by God. She also began to pray more often and found that it helped her feel more at peace and connected to God.

God's Unconditional Love and Forgiveness

One of the most important aspects of building a relationship with God is understanding that He loves us unconditionally and offers us forgiveness and grace, even when we make mistakes. Children who struggle with behavioral problems may feel guilty or ashamed of their actions, but it is important for them to know that God loves them regardless of their mistakes.

One example of this is the story of a boy named John who was struggling with addiction. He had made many mistakes and felt like he had let down his family and friends. However, after turning to God and seeking help, he found comfort in knowing that God loved him and forgave him for his mistakes. This gave him the strength to overcome his addiction and start a new, healthier life.

Be an active member of a church.

Church is the family of God. In church, God is the father, every other person in the church just like you are his children. In the house of God, there is fullness of joy. When you spend time with the people of God, you will get to know God more, you will also learn to relate with people very well.

Bill was used to live a very lonely life; his best friends were his video games and pets. But Scot who is new in the neighborhood invited him to church. Ever since he started going to church, he has been living a happy life and he connects with people better. Bill is now grateful to God for filling his life with joy, peace, goodness, and good people.

Chapter 5: Turning Your Behavior Around with God's Help

Behavior reflects our inner self, and sometimes, we may struggle with making the right choices or behaving appropriately. However, with God's help, we can turn our behavior around and become better versions of ourselves. In this chapter, we will discuss practical advice for how kids can turn their behavior around with God's help; identify positive behaviors that reflect the love and grace of God, the importance of forgiveness, and why kids should seek out positive role models and mentors.

Practical Advice for Turning Your Behavior Around with God's Help

When we are struggling with our behavior, it can be challenging to know where to start in turning things around. However, the Bible offers some practical advice for how we can improve our behavior with God's help. One of the key things we can do is to focus on our thoughts. The Bible tells us in Philippians 4:8 to think about things that are true, noble, right, pure, lovely, admirable, excellent, and praiseworthy. By focusing on these things, we can start to change our mindset and make better choices.

Another practical step is to pray and ask God for guidance and strength. We can ask God to help us overcome our weaknesses and give us the strength to make better choices. Additionally, we can read the Bible and seek out passages that speak to our specific struggles. By doing so, we can find comfort and guidance in God's word.

We can also read the Bible and look for stories of people who turned their lives around with God's help, such as Paul the Apostle or Mary Magdalene.

Another step is to take responsibility for our actions and seek forgiveness when we make mistakes. It can be hard to admit when we have done something wrong, but it is a crucial step in turning our behavior around. We should also seek to make amends with those we have hurt.

Forgiveness is another important aspect of turning our behavior around. We need to not only seek forgiveness from others, but also forgive ourselves for past mistakes. When we forgive others, and ourselves we can move forward and make positive changes.

Identifying Positive Behaviors That Reflect the Love and Grace of God

God's love and grace are unconditional, and as His followers, we should strive to reflect these qualities in our behavior. Positive behaviors that reflect God's love and grace include kindness, compassion, forgiveness, and generosity. By showing these qualities to others, we can create a positive impact and inspire those around us to do the same.

When we behave positively, it not only reflects our relationship with God but also shows that we are actively trying to be better people. We should focus on being intentional in our actions, making sure that our behavior aligns with the love and grace of God.

The Importance of Forgiveness, Both of Oneself and Of Others

Forgiveness is an essential aspect of our relationship with God and others. It allows us to let go of negative emotions and move forward with a positive mindset. As kids, it can be hard to understand why forgiveness is so important. However, the Bible tells us that forgiveness is not only necessary but also a requirement for our own salvation.

We should strive to forgive others, just as God forgives us. We can do this by letting go of grudges and choosing to focus on the positive qualities of others. Additionally, we should also learn to forgive ourselves when we make mistakes. It is important to remember that we are all imperfect and will make mistakes, but with God's help, we can learn from them and move forward.

Seeking Out Positive Role Models and Mentors

Finally, seeking out positive role models and mentors can be incredibly helpful in turning our behavior around. By surrounding ourselves with people who embody positive behaviors, we can learn from them and be inspired to make positive changes in our own lives. It is important to choose role models who align with our values and who can offer guidance and support when we need it.

Mentors can also be beneficial in helping us navigate difficult situations and providing advice and guidance when we need it. A mentor can be a parent, teacher, coach, or another trusted adult in our lives. It is important to be open and honest with our mentors, and to seek their guidance and support when we need it.

Volunteering and Serving Others

One way to turn our behavior around is by volunteering and serving others. By helping those in need, we are reflecting God's love and grace. Volunteering can also help us develop a sense of purpose and boost our self-esteem. We can seek out opportunities to volunteer at local charities, hospitals, or places of worship.

Remember to be patient, seek forgiveness, and trust in God's plan for your life.

Chapter 6: Building Healthy Habits

We are glad you have made it this far. If you want to be strong and healthy, both physically and mentally, it is important to develop healthy habits that will help you live a happy and fulfilling life. Let us dive in and learn more about building healthy habits!

The Importance of Developing Healthy Habits

Developing healthy habits is essential for our physical and mental well-being. When we take care of our bodies, we feel better and have more energy to do the things we love. In addition, when we take care of our minds, we feel happier and more at peace. Developing healthy habits is all about taking care of ourselves so that we can be the best version of ourselves.

Strategies for Developing Healthy Habits

There are many strategies you can use to develop healthy habits. **Here are some practical tips to get you started:**

Prayer: Spending time in prayer can help you connect with God and find peace and strength in Him. Prayer helps you to receive good emotions from God. It also gives you strength to withstand any challenge or negative situation that might come your way.

Meditating on God's word: Reading and reflecting on God's word can help you stay focused on what is important and find guidance for your life. When you equip yourself with God's word, you will have the right responses to every situation even before they happen. God's word is God's wisdom, it will make you wise.

Forgiveness: Forgiving others and you is an essential part of developing healthy habits. It helps us let go of negative emotions and move forward with a positive attitude.

When you forgive yourself and other people also, you will be free from offences and negativity.

Benevolence: Helping others is a great way to develop healthy habits. It brings joy to both the person you are helping and yourself. When you practice benevolence, you are reflecting God's character to other people. It will get rid or ill-will in your relationship with people.

Self-control: Practicing self-control is essential for developing healthy habits. It helps us resist temptation and make positive choices. Self-control means to delay immediate gratification for a more noble purpose. When you practice self-control, you will e disciplined.

Obedience to God: Following God's commands helps us develop healthy habits that align with His will for our lives. When you are obedient to God, you will live a fulfilled life, it will make you always satisfied.

Peace resolution: Resolving conflicts peacefully is crucial for our mental health and well-being. It helps us maintain positive relationships and avoid unnecessary stress. The bible says blessed are the peacemakers for they shall see God.

Exercise: Regular physical activity helps us stay fit and healthy. It also releases endorphins, which are natural mood boosters.

Healthy eating: Eating a balanced and nutritious diet is essential for our physical and mental well-being. It provides us with the nutrients we need to function at our best.

Good sleep habits: Getting enough sleep is crucial for our health and well-being. It helps us feel rested and refreshed, so we can tackle each day with energy and enthusiasm.

Emulate good examples: When you see someone doing good things, copy that example.

Communicate: Most of the troubles we face at home and in social interactions stem misunderstanding. When there is communication breakdown, both parties cannot understand each other, consequently one might start throwing tantrums to get the attention needed.

Managing Negative Behaviors

Sometimes, we may find ourselves struggling with negative behaviors such as anger, jealousy, or pride. Here are some strategies to help you manage these negative behaviors:

Mindful of God's word: Reading and reflecting on God's word can help us stay grounded in His truth and resist negative influences.

Shunning negative influences: Avoiding negative influences such as bad company or harmful media can help us maintain a positive mindset and avoid negative behaviors.

Self-discipline: Practicing self-discipline is key to managing negative behaviors. It helps us resist temptation and make positive choices.

Motivation: Staying motivated and focused on our goals is essential for overcoming negative behaviors and developing healthy habits.

Remember, building healthy habits takes time and effort, but the rewards are worth it. With God's help and your determination, you can develop healthy habits that will help you live a happy and fulfilling life.

Chapter 7: Creating a Plan for Change

In this chapter, we are going to talk about creating a plan for change. Sometimes, we know we need to change our behavior, but we are not quite sure where to start. That is where a plan comes in handy!

The first thing to remember is that your plan should be realistic and achievable. You do not want to set yourself up for failure by creating a plan that is too difficult to follow. Instead, start with small steps that you know you can handle. For example, if you want to stop yelling at your siblings, start by practicing taking deep breaths and counting to ten before reacting.

Once you have your goal in mind, it is important to break it down into smaller steps. This makes it easier to accomplish and helps you see progress along the way. For example, if your goal is to be more organized with your schoolwork, you can break it down by creating a study schedule, setting up a designated study area, and making a to-do list for each day.

Staying motivated and accountable is also crucial for making progress. Find ways to keep yourself motivated, such as rewarding yourself for reaching milestones or finding a friend or family member to check in with you regularly. It can also be helpful to track your progress, such as with a chart or journal, so you can see how far you have come.

Here are some practical steps for creating a plan for behavior change:

Step 1: Identify the behavior you want to change. This could be something like being more organized, being kinder to others, or stopping a bad habit like lying.

Step 2: Set a realistic and achievable goal. Remember to break it down into smaller steps to make it easier to accomplish.

Step 3: Identify your triggers. What situations or emotions cause you to engage in the behavior you want to change? Understanding your triggers can help you be more mindful of your actions and prevent slipping back into old habits.

Step 4: Develop a plan for dealing with your triggers. This could be as simple as taking a deep breath and counting to ten before reacting, or finding a healthy outlet for your emotions like going for a walk or talking to a trusted friend or family member.

Step 5: Find ways to stay motivated and accountable. This could be rewarding yourself for reaching milestones, finding a friend or family member to check in with you regularly, or tracking your progress with a chart or journal.

Remember, making behavior changes takes time and effort. Be patient with yourself and celebrate your successes along the way. Moreover, do not forget to ask God for help and guidance in your journey towards becoming the best version of yourself.

Bonus Chapter

Creating a 21-days Calendar for Behavior Change by Aligning with God

Hello children! We hope you have enjoyed reading this book and have learned a lot about how to align your behavior with God's plan for your life. In this final chapter, we will show you how to create a month calendar to help you stick to your behavior change plan.

First, choose a goal that you want to achieve. It could be something like being more patient, being kinder to others or studying harder in school. Then, write it down on a piece of paper and put it somewhere you will see it every day, like on your bedroom wall or your fridge.

Next, break down your goal into smaller steps that you can take each day. For example, if your goal is to be more example, if your goal is to be more patient, you could start by taking a deep breath and counting to 10 whenever you feel frustrated. On the other hand, if your goal is to study harder in school, you could set aside 30 minutes each day to review your notes.

Once you have your smaller steps, create a calendar for the month and write down each step on the corresponding day. Make sure you leave some room for unexpected things that may come up, like a family event or a school project.

As you go through the month, check off each step as you complete it. This will help you stay motivated and accountable for your progress. Remember, changing your behavior is not easy, but with God's help, anything is possible.

Week 1:

Day 1: Start the day with prayer and reflection on God's word. Set an intention for the day, such as being kind to others or avoiding negative behaviors.

Day 2: Focus on forgiveness, of both you and others. Consider who you need to forgive and pray for the strength to do so.

Day 3: Practice benevolence by performing an act of kindness for someone else. It can be as simple as holding the door open or offering a kind word.

Day 4: Reflect on self-control and practice it in challenging situations. Think about a behavior you struggle with and focus on resisting the temptation to engage in that behavior.

Day 5: Take time to rest and prioritize your mental and physical health. Consider taking a break from social media or technology and engaging in a relaxing activity like reading or spending time in nature.

Day 6: Focus on obedience to God and His teachings. Think about how you can live a life that is pleasing to God.

Day 7: Attend a church service or engage in a spiritual activity that brings you closer to God.

Week 2:

Day 8: Start the day with prayer and reflection on God's word. Set an intention for the day that aligns with your goals for behavior change.

Day 9: Focus on self-reflection and identifying areas of your behavior that need improvement. Write down your reflections in a journal, discuss them with a trusted friend, or mentor.

Day 10: Practice peace resolution by resolving any conflicts or disagreements you may have with others. Consider apologizing or reaching out to make amends.

Day 11: Focus on practicing self-control in difficult situations. Take a deep breath and focus on your goals for behavior change when you feel tempted to engage in negative behaviors.

Day 12: Reflect on God's grace and forgiveness, and how you can extend that to others. Consider reaching out to someone, you may have hurt in the past to apologize and seek forgiveness.

Day 13: Focus on living a life that is obedient to God's teachings. Think about how you can be a positive influence in the world and spread love and kindness.

Day 14: Attend a church service or engage in a spiritual activity that brings you closer to God.

Week 3:

Day 15: Start the day with prayer and reflection on God's word. Set an intention for the day that aligns with your goals for behavior change.

Day 16: Focus on forgiveness and how you can extend it to yourself. Write down affirmations or positive messages to remind yourself of your worth and value in God's eyes.

Day 17: Practice benevolence by volunteering or performing an act of kindness for someone in need.

Day 18: Focus on practicing self-control in challenging situations. Take a deep breath and focus on your goals for behavior change when you feel tempted to engage in negative behaviors.

Day 19: Reflect on the importance of rest and prioritizing your mental and physical health. Take time to engage in self-care activities that bring you joy and relaxation.

Day 20: Focus on living a life that is obedient to God's teachings. Think about how you can be a positive influence in the world and spread love and kindness.

Day 21: Attend a church service or engage in a spiritual activity that brings you closer to God.

Conclusion

Congratulations, young readers! You have made it to the end of this book, "Aligning Your Behavior with God's Plan." We hope that you have gained some valuable insights on how to align your behavior with God's plan for your life.

In this book, we have discussed the importance of understanding God's plan for your life, building a relationship with Him, turning your behavior around with His help, and developing healthy habits. We have also provided practical advice on how to create a plan for change that is realistic and achievable.

Remember, God loves you unconditionally and wants the best for you. He has a unique plan for your life that only you can fulfill. By aligning your behavior with His plan, you will experience a sense of purpose, fulfillment, and joy.

We encourage you to seek out support from trusted adults or mentors as you work on improving your behavior and developing a deeper relationship with God. You can also turn to additional resources, such as your church, youth group, or counseling services, for guidance on behavior management and spiritual development.

Always remember that change is possible with God's help. Keep praying, reading His word, and seeking His guidance. And most importantly, always believe in yourself and the amazing plan God has for your life.

References And Research were taken from here:

C. (2021, January 26). *What is ADHD?* Centers for Disease Control and Prevention.
https://www.cdc.gov/ncbddd/adhd/facts.html

Definition of BEHAVIOR. (2023, March 22). Behavior Definition & Meaning - Merriam-Webster.
https://www.merriam-webster.com/dictionary/behavior

Definition of EMOTION. (2023, March 22). Emotion Definition & Meaning - Merriam-Webster.
https://www.merriam-webster.com/dictionary/emotion

Robinson, M. (2023, March 26). *How to Stop Being Scared of Emotions - ITS PSYCHOLOGY*. How to Stop Being Scared of Emotions - ITS PSYCHOLOGY. https://itspsychology.com/scared-of-emotions/

9 Simple Habits for a Healthier Lifestyle. (2023, March 27). TASEYNN. https://www.taseynn.com/2023/03/9-simple-habits-for-healthier-lifestyle.html

Depression for Orlando, FL and Seattle, WA | Breakthrough HQ | Psychiatry. (n.d.). Depression for Orlando, FL and Seattle, WA | Breakthrough HQ | Psychiatry. https://www.breakthroughhq.com/service/depression

Nambiar, H. (2023, March 12). *Forgiving Others: How to Find Inner Peace and Happiness*. Medium. https://medium.com/a-smiling-world/forgiving-others-how-to-find-

inner-peace-and-happiness-
5d91f4091045

www.ingramcontent.com/pod-product-compliance
Lightning Source LLC
Chambersburg PA
CBHW061601250726

48657CB00020B/853